The 12 Basic Skills of FLY FISHING

Woolly Bugger

The 12 Basic Skills of FLY FISHING

Ted Peck & Ed Rychkun

hancock house

ISBN 0-88839-392-X
Copyright © 1996 Ted Peck, Ed Rychkun

Second printing 2004

Cataloging in Publication Data
Peck, Ted, 1929–
    The 12 basic skills of fly fishing

    ISBN 0-88839-392-X

    1. Fly fishing. 2. Fly casting. I. Rychkun, Ed. II. Title.
III. Title: Twelve basic skills of fly fishing.
SH456.P42 1996   799.1'2   C96-910197-X

Editing: Nancy Miller
Production: Nancy Miller, Myron Shutty, Ed Rychkun
Cover photos: Ted Peck with student Robyn Eha. Photos taken by Ed Rychkun.

Published simultaneously in Canada and the United States by

HANCOCK HOUSE PUBLISHERS LTD.
19313 Zero Avenue, Surrey, B.C. V3S 9R9
(604) 538-1114 Fax (604) 538-2262

HANCOCK HOUSE PUBLISHERS
1431 Harrison Avenue, Blaine, WA 98230-5005
(604) 538-1114 Fax (604) 538-2262
Web Site: www.hancockhouse.com *Email:* sales@hancockhouse.com

Contents

Acknowledgments

I have spent most of my life dedicated to the art of sport fishing. It has been both my vocation and my avocation for many years. For the last decade I have kept close to the art by teaching people the simple, basic skills of fishing that I have spent more than half a century learning and refining, so others could also find enjoyment. But many things have changed. The equipment, and certainly the technology available, has altered and improved dramatically, even though the basics remain the same. I still, however, needed to bring these skills into the context of modern day technology. For this I would like to acknowledge the valuable support of Jay Mailey, proprietor of Jaymer's Fishing Tackle in Port Coquitlam. He not only encouraged me to write this manual, but has been instrumental in helping me adapt my experience to modern technology.

I would also like to acknowledge the support of my wife Luba, who was able to convert my scratchy notes into readable form. It is through her encouragement and relentless support that these basic skills have materialized to be shared with others.

Finally, without the needling and gentle but firm pushing from extremely knowledgeable outdoors author, former student and fellow sport fishing enthusiast Ed Rychkun, this simple volume would never have left my head to be transferred to paper.

Ted Peck

Royal Coachman

6

Preface

I first got to know Ted through his night classes. Being an avid angler myself, I was always interested in that extra tidbit of information that someone else could offer, particularly from someone who was known to be an expert. The name Ted Peck had always been synonymous with fishing expertise for me and many others who grew up during the 1940s. Ted was always on radio or television tantalizing anglers with a few of his new found secrets.

Since my experience in fishing had focused more on dragging hardware around the interior lakes, I never paid much attention to fly fishing. Like many others, I believed the art of fly fishing was indeed an art, reserved for those who had the time to learn what seemed a bit complicated...a fine craft reserved for a different breed of experts. But I decided to capture a few hours and take Ted's course. In the back of my mind was that image of fly fishing...one of enormous books bulging with information on techniques, entomology (study of bugs), "matching hatches" and endless technological variations of tackle...on tippets, on lines, this knot, that knot, sinking, floating, dry, wet, etc., etc., etc. And then there was the execution: roll cast, back cast, mending, stripping. How could any normal mortal have enough recreation time to learn this stuff?

As I sat conscientiously and listened to this stern-looking gentleman, I noted that he would inject jokes and fish stories in the lecture. As I looked at my sparse notes, I began to wonder how he was going to teach us all I expected to learn in two hours. Ted's time was running out and at half time he had probably spent only about half an hour on this complicated topic. By this time we had covered half of his 12 basic skills. "Was this it?" I asked myself.

The truth was that Ted had, over many years, reduced the whole process to its very fundamental roots. It was me that was confused, not Ted. He stripped away the complications by teaching what were the most effective tactics. He had refined these strategies by using new technology in tackle, thereby making the process even simpler. These secrets he had put together in some scratchy notes that only he could read. He called these the 12 basic skills.

When we took a break, I began to realize exactly what these skills were. Within one hour the whole class had learned to assemble the tackle and execute a real cast...in the parking lot. What amazed me was how Ted cut through the maze to get rid of all the mystique and complexity that had been bugging me...all in just one hour!

I still had my doubts, however, in that this was all very cool, but what about execution? What about getting the line out? What about catching fish? Well, the second surprise came at the field session at Buntzen Lake. It took only a few hours and the whole class was casting, in graceful fluid arcs. We had learned to execute roll, false and straight forward casts. We could strip, mend line, tie knots and we all had assembled our own tackle. Now we could make sense of the whole process. We were ready for the real stuff.

Over the years, Ted had cleverly reduced everything to incredible simplicity. Like so many things in life, the most difficult problem is to make things uncomplicated. Ted's teachings were simple, but the years of experience required to reduce the process was anything but. Ted eliminated all the variations. He was not concerned about "if this, then that" routines on equipment and tackle. He avoided trying to provide information to be able to fish every situation in every environment. Ted was concerned with getting a person started, not trying to give a person a Ph.D. in Fishology. The mission was to get people to understand and apply the basics…quickly, so the art could be enjoyed. Ted gives the basic techniques so one can technically perform the strokes. Refining the art form becomes the individual's future challenge.

It is amazing how effective this process is, the size of this book should be certain evidence of this.

Ed Rychkun

Werner Shrimp

Introduction

Long before there existed the town of Whistler, the Sea to Sky Highway, or the BC Rail line from North Vancouver to Prince George and beyond, there was Alta Lake. More specifically there was Rainbow Lodge, located on the northwest shore of Alta Lake. The only mode of transportation in those days was the Union Steamship company and the PGE Railway, allowing travel by sea from Vancouver, up Howe Sound to Squamish dock, then by rail between Squamish dock and Quesnel.

It was by the above travel methods, beginning in 1938, that my granddad treated me every spring to a four-day visit to Rainbow Lodge. It was here that he introduced me to the fascinating world of trout fishing. The lodge was owned and operated by Alec and Myrtle Philip, as capable, as well as hospitable, a couple as I ever met.

In the spring of 1940, Mrs. Philip took me under her wing and, in the space of less than two days, taught me to fly fish. On a T-shaped float near what she termed her "trout nursery" she had me casting among the lily pads with a Royal Coachman fly. In short order she taught me not only to cast, but also how to hook, play and release trout. The lessons stand out in my memory because, on that occasion, one of my 6-10 inch rainbows wound itself around a lily pad stem. Suddenly, swiftly and silently, a grayish green, huge fish lunged from the deep water onto the shoal and, before my eyes, ate my trout with one gulp!

With Mrs. Philip's instruction and the aid of a long-handled landing net hastily fetched from the nearby horse barn, I was able to land an eleven-pound Dolly Varden char before my eleventh birthday. From that spring day fifty-five years ago, I was hooked on fly fishing.

During my teen years, fly fishing took a back burner position to other angling pursuits. By 1945, salmon fishing, in all its forms, occupied 50 percent of my fishing time. Steelhead trout float fishing also captured me. A retired dentist today, but then a keen and knowledgeable steelheader, introduced me to the many arts and skills of how to outwit the wiliest of the sea-run trout of B.C. His name is David Leonard McNair. That summer of 1945, while working as a field assistant for the Department of Fisheries and Oceans on the Bulkley River at Moricetown, and thanks to Dave's teachings, I landed a 29 lb. 14 oz. steelhead.

As I entered UBC in 1946, fly fishing emerged again, consisting of forays to local beaches, streams, lakes and sloughs. The spreading knowledge of what a wrapping of feathers, fur, tinsel, hair and thread around a hook can create still impresses me. Artificial flies imitating full-grown insects illustrated by books and magazines are only one-fifth of the types of food consumed by trout and other game fish. A few examples of a more complete diet would include shrimps, both fresh and salt water varieties, immature insects, worms, salmon roe, single eggs, small fish, leeches, and even small frogs, mice and voles.

During both the summers of 1948 and 1949, my fly fishing abilities were again called upon by a fishing lodge northeast of Kamloops where I was employed as a guide. It was here that I taught many well-heeled Californians and in doing so developed what I call, for want of a better name, the 12 basic skills of fly fishing.

Ted Peck

Woolly Worm

Skill 1
Selection of Equipment

The first and most fundamental of all of the 12 skills is the selection and assembly of your fly fishing equipment. You will need a rod, a reel and a floating weight forward line. The line will be identified by a code and a number which matches, or exceeds by one number, the AFTMA (American Fishing Tackle Manufacturers Association) size line printed on your rod forward of the cork handle. An AFTMA number indicates that the rod is "technologically engineered" to best accommodate the size line with the same number. Average fishing situations will call for a 6 or 7 to start with. This will let you have an end line strength of around 6 pounds, good enough for a healthy fish fight, and that covers most situations. If you were after steelhead for example, the choice would be a 9. The rod should also have a minimum of nine guides to hold the line. The more guides there are the easier it is for the line to slide out.

Fly rods come in many lengths and actions. By actions, I mean "whippiness." The stiffer the rod, the better it is for dry fly fishing; the softer the rod, as in the action of a buggy whip, the better for wet fly fishing. When learning, pick out a medium action 8 ft. 6 in., 9 ft. or 9 ft. 6 in. rod, preferably graphite with a cork handle. These graphite rods will typically be in the $80 to $110 price range.

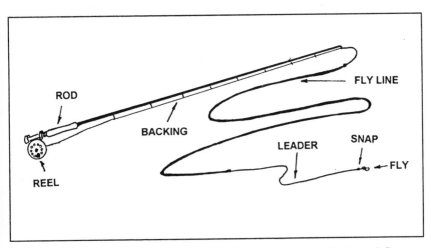

Basic equipment: rod, reel, backing, fly line, leader, snap hook and fly.

Fly reels are simple, single-action, center-pin devices that are used to both store the line and backing, as well as to play large fish. In choosing one, make sure spare spools are available for it, because as you progress in your fishing, you will require several speeds of sinking lines i.e., fast, medium and slow, as well

11

as at least one line with a sink tip. These lines are designed to sink into the water at different speeds. A reel with spare spools will allow you to snap other lines onto the reel easily.

Backing line is next. You will need 50 yards of 20-pound test soft backing line made of braided nylon or dacron. This connects the reel to the fly line.

The next item you need is fly line. Floating, weight-forward fly line should be used to learn with. This is symbolized by the code WF-6-F (weight-forward floating line). The weight of 6 will match your rod. The code is found on the fly line box. It is a standard format with meaning:

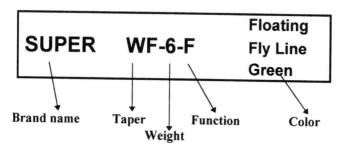

The taper codes are WF for weight forward, DT for double taper, L for level, BBT for bass bug taper, SWT for saltwater taper and so on. The function codes are F for floating, S for sinking, F/S for floating/sinking and so on.

Leader is attached to the end of the fly line. You will need a tapered, monofilament nylon leader, not to exceed the length of your rod, which is around 9 feet. Start with size 3X, 5-7 pound test at the tip, about 9 feet long.

Snap hooks are the final part of the assembly. These come in a small package. A snap hook is a little piece of spring steel, size 1-2-3, which is tied to the end of the leader. Always select the smallest size available.

Finally, at the end of the line, you have what this whole process is meant to accommodate a fly. Flies are simply snapped on or off.

You are now ready to assemble all this equipment in the second basic skill.

Skill 2
Assembly of Tackle

The second skill is the correct assembly of your tackle. The tackle is brought together by using two "knots" and two "splices" tied in the positions shown below. In reality, as you can see, the same knot and splice is used twice, greatly simplifying the process of assembly.

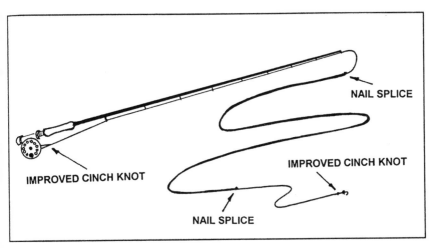

Assembly of tackle using the improved cinch knot and the nail splice.

The first step is to attach the backing to the reel. The backing serves two purposes. First, it provides extra line, giving you an extra 50 yards to play a large fish. Second, the extra line fills out the reel drum to allow the fly line to leave the drum easier.

Tying the backing to the reel is done by using an **improved cinch knot**. To do this, the end of the backing is tied around the center of the reel or drum that the line will be wound on. This is a simple knot done as follows:

13

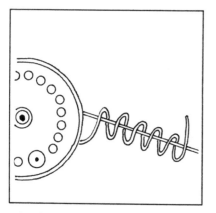 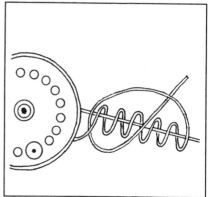

1. Slip the end of the line around the reel drum and wrap the end around the main line away from the reel for 5 turns.

2. Push the end back through the opening between the reel. Poke the end through the large open loop and snug lightly around the main line.

3. Pull slowly on the main line until the loosely tied knot slides down snugly around the drum and clip off the extra piece.

Now you need to wind the backing onto the reel. As you wind, make sure the line feeds into the reel properly in the right direction. You should get used to reeling with the right hand. Make tight smooth layers across the drum, alternating slowly from one side to the other as you wind it in. After you finish reeling all but the last five feet onto the reel, get ready to splice the backing to the fly line.

You must now learn the basic splice that joins the backing to the fly line and fly line to the leader. Lately there has been a tool developed called a Tie-Fast that makes the process simple and easy. The reason that splices rather than knots are employed is that knots stick in the rod guides and splices shoot through with ease.

The Tie-Fast is essentially helping to tie a **nail splice.** If you do not have such a device, you would be tying the **nailless splice** (or knot). In either case the process is the same, the device just makes it easier. You should practice tying this splice to become proficient.

First, we must connect the end of the backing to the start of the fly line. Be careful to locate the butt end of the fly line, which is usually marked with a sticker or tag indicating so, then handle it carefully to avoid a tangle.

14

The splice is made by following the steps below:

1. Place the Tie-Fast in palm of either hand and grasp tightly with fingers as shown in the picture for step 3 below. Place the thumb on the thumb pad. The tip should be in perfect focus.

2. Place the backing line over and through the channel and then through the tines at the front end of the tool. It should extend out about 10 inches downward past the end of the slot. Use the thumb to secure the line over the pad.

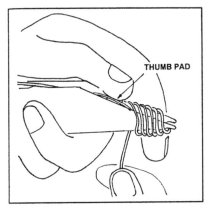

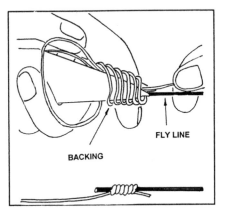

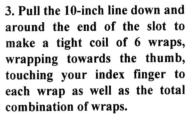

3. Pull the 10-inch line down and around the end of the slot to make a tight coil of 6 wraps, wrapping towards the thumb, touching your index finger to each wrap as well as the total combination of wraps.

4. After you make the last wrap, take the end of the backing and thread it back into the channel under the turns and out through the slot. Now you have two ends of backing to cinch tight around the fly line. Insert the fly line into the groove.

5. Once the line backing is through and the fly line is in place, pull the backing tight slowly, then give it a light jerk. This causes the splice to slide off onto the fly line. Now pull the two lines until the splice is snug. Trim off excess, and don't worry about making the ends too short. This splice only gets tighter by pulling.

Once you have completed this process you can reel in the fly line, making tight smooth layers across the top of the backing, alternating slowly from one side to the other as you wind it in. Then put the sticker from the fly line box on the *inside* of the reel spool so you don't forget what it is.

15

The next step is to connect the leader to the end of the fly line using the same splice. Make sure that if you are using a tapered leader, the thicker end is the one you wrap with. Follow the same instructions as above.

The last part of the assembly involves tying the fly to the end of the fly line. This is done by using an improved cinch knot. This is the same knot used to tie the backing onto the reel. One of the more simple but effective inventions is the snap hook, used to snap flies on or off the end of the line. This prevents shortening your leader every time you change flies.

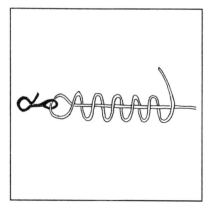 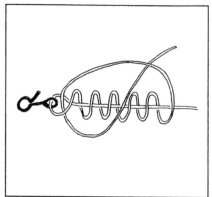

1. Insert the end of the leader through the eye and wrap the end around the main line away from the eye for 6 turns.

2. Push the end back through the opening between the eye and the first loop. Poke the end through the larger open loop and pull.

3. Hold the eye in one hand and pull the tie end slightly until the knot begins to close. Pull it secure and trim the end.

The next part of the assembly process requires putting the rod and reel together with the connected line. Most modern graphite fly rods consist of only two sections, the butt and the tip. There are no metal ferrules to stick and rust, as there were on the old split cane and some fiberglass rods. Simply push the two sections together but not quite all the way. Now, holding the rod by the cork handle up to your master eye, guides up, sight down the guides, like a rifle, to make sure all are perfectly aligned.

If the guides are even slightly misaligned, it will cause wear on them as well as damage to your line, not to mention difficulty in casting, as the line will not pass through the guides easily. This will result in a very tired wrist. Now push both sections completely together. The next step is to make sure your reel is securely locked on to the rod at the reel seat. Now pull out the leader to where it is spliced to the line, kink the join and string it through all the guides horizontally, pulling the remaining leader and about ten feet of line after the kinked join has been pulled past the rod tip. To make a kink in the line at the join, you simply fold it and push the fold through the guides to the end of the rod tip. Note that you will save yourself a lot of frustration if you do this while the rod is held horizontally. This keeps the line from falling out onto the ground out of the guides.

Water Boatman

Skill 3
Holding the Fly Rod

You are now ready to learn the third skill, which is how to hold the fly rod. The first step is to find the balance point. This is accomplished by placing your index finger exactly in front of where the cork handle meets the graphite. The rod, reel and line will react in one of three ways. The reel end will dip lower in which case it is **butt heavy**. If the rod tip dips then it is **nose heavy**. If the rod remains level then it is **balanced**. The objective is to move your index finger to a point where the rod is balanced. It is at this imaginary point that you will place the tip of your thumb when grasping the rod.

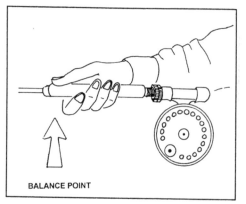

BALANCE POINT

Place the thumb at the balance point.

If the assembly is balanced, place your casting hand with your thumb in line with the rod exactly on the forward edge of the cork handle. If you do not hold the rod at the balance point, your casting arm, wrist and hand will tire unnecessarily.

Marabou Leech

Skill 4
Mastering the Roll Cast

Skill number four involves mastering the first of three casts. It is called the roll cast. The function of this procedure is twofold: first, when you are fishing in a situation where trees, bushes or a high stream bank are immediately behind you, thereby making any line movement to your rear impossible, you are restricted to casting forward of your arm and wrist, the roll cast makes this possible.

Second, the roll cast is employed to straighten out messes and line coils in front of you when they occur. A good example of this is the missed or aborted strike. Each time a trout takes your fly, spits it out or breaks it off your leader, a mess is created when you quickly raise your rod tip to hook the fish. This mess must be straightened out before commencing a subsequent forward cast, which I will explain later.

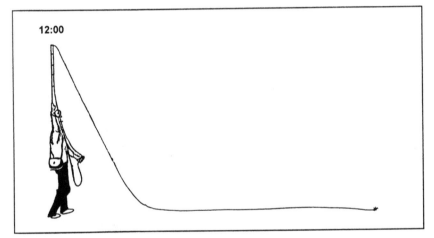

1. With line straight out in front, raise the rod to 12:00.

The mechanics of the roll cast are as follows. Simply raise your casting arm and rod as high as possible to the 12:00 position on an imaginary clock and cant your wrist slightly away from your body, to the side. **The convention used is to always consider 9:00 as the position of your rod at the final cast, or delivery. Thus no matter what direction you face, the imaginary clock rotates with you.**

Make sure that there is no backward motion to the line in front of you. In other words, an absolutely still line is essential before executing the cast. The cast is executed by holding the rod in the casting hand and the fly line between thumb

19

and forefinger of the free hand. This allows you to control the way the line is released or pulled off the reel. You will first learn to cast by simply holding the line firm. Later you will learn to feed it out from this position.

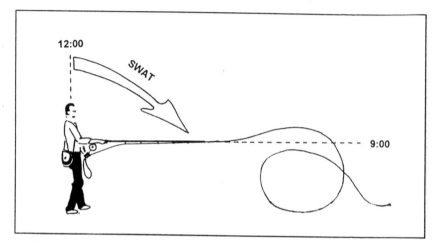

2. Swat the rod sharply from 12:00 to 9:00.

Your next move is to whip the rod in a sharp downward motion from 12:00 down to 9:00, or even 8:30 when you are a beginner. The key word I use with all my students, whether in organized classes or one on one, is **swat** and **s**wat with authority! If the cast is executed correctly you will see the line roll over on itself and straighten right out. The fly will not catch on the line because you have canted your wrist, rod and line away from your body. With practice you will soon be roll casting from 30 to 45 yards with ease.

EXERCISE

You should now take your assembled tackle, find an open area and practice this 12:00 to 9:00 action until it is a comfortable operation and you are able to roll 30 to 45 yards of line out in a graceful rolling action. It should end up perfectly straight in front of you.

Skill 5
Mastering the False Cast

Skill number five is the false cast. It is thusly named because the line leader and fly do not touch the water. During the cast the line stays in the air, both in front of and behind your body. This cast has three main uses: first, it facilitates the taking of line from the reel at the commencement of fishing. Second, when having retrieved a sinking or sink tip line from the water, it is used to get the line out to the fish again.

Third, when dry fly fishing over fish rising to the surface, you are three quarters of the way to reaching rising trout within range by having your line in the air.

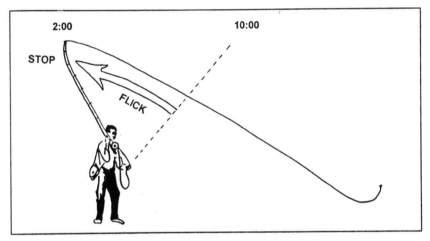

1. Start at 10:00 then flick the rod to 2:00 and stop.

The clock position to start a false cast is 10:00. Make sure that the line is straight out in front of you so that it lifts uniformly as you begin the initial back stroke. If the line is bent or curled the backward motion will not be a consistent pull. Then with a deft flick of the wrist the rod tip travels to 2:00. It is important to remember that this cast is not a fluid motion. By flicking to 2:00 and stopping, the momentum of the line continues its flight back behind you in a round arc. The reason for the stop is to give the line a few seconds to form the arc behind you, setting it up for the next flick and stop at 10:00.

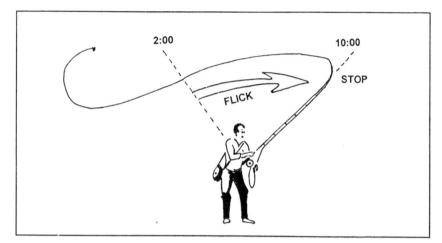

2. Flick the rod to 10:00 and stop.

The key words to learn by are 10 to 2, **flick** and **stop**. Once again, the line will now arc in front of you after you stop at 10:00. As the arc forms, you flick back to 2:00 again in a flick-and-stop pattern. Although your motion is not fluid, the line motion will become fluid.

It is in the forward motion that you will let more line out. This is done by holding the line between forefinger and thumb of the free hand and pulling about two feet of line off the reel on the 10:00 to 2:00 backward motion. The slack line, called **stripped off line**, is between the reel and your finger so it is not released on the back flick. It does not matter when you pull line off the reel, but it is vitally imperative that you do not release that stripped off line you are now holding in your free hand until the rod is at least 10:00. By releasing the stripped line on the forward motion, then stripping more line on the back motion, you get more and more line in the air.

After several false casts, when you wish to finally lay the line down on the water, the rod must be stopped at 9:00. The flatter the rod when you release line from your hand, the faster and smoother the line shoots through the guides.

EXERCISES

It is important to practice the casting process until you are able to get more and more line in the air and further out. You should start with a short amount of about 10 yards and work up to 30 to 40 yards. Find an open field, or better still an open shoreline, and practice the following exercises:

1. Execute a roll cast to get about 10 yards of line out in front of you. Your rod should be pointed out parallel to the line. From a rod position of 8:30, pick up the line on a backstroke and begin the 10:00 to 2:00 false cast motion, keeping the line in the air to develop the flick-and-stop motion.

2. Practice by placing about 10 yards of line in front of you and flick up to 2:00 to get the false cast underway. Continue the flick-and-stop sequence until the line, not the arm motion, is making a smooth rolling arc. Then on the upstroke pull out about 18 inches of line with the free hand. Release this at the end of the forward motion at 10:00 to get more line in the air. Make sure that you do not begin the flick back until the stripped line has "shot" out. Let another 10 yards out this way, then on the final stop at 9:00 let the final amount of a few feet shoot out for the final delivery. Do this until you are comfortable.

3. Try executing a roll cast to get about 15 yards of line in front of you. Just as it completes the roll, flick the line up into a false cast and get another 10 yards of line out by stripping. Try to get as much line in the air as possible before making the final release. You will begin to develop a special sense of timing as you stop for a short pause before each flick, letting the line complete its smooth arc each time.

Doc Spratley

Skill 6
Mastering the Straight Forward Cast

Skill number six consists of using the basic cast you will use most often, with several variations, for the rest of your life. It is simply called the forward or sometimes straight forward cast. The rod travels from 8:30 to 1:00 making sure, before you cast, that there is no kink or bend in the line in front of the rod tip. If this occurs, the rod is not effective in lifting the line until it reaches 10:00 or 11:00, and as it stops at 1:00, it conveys very little power to the line as you flick it down to 9:00 or even 8:30.

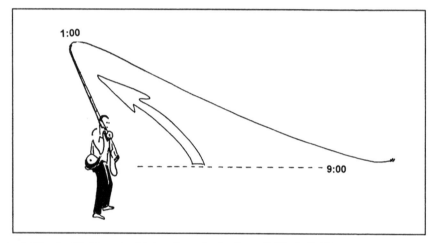

1. Start with line straight and upstroke from 9:00 to 1:00.

When learning the forward cast, put more power on the up stroke to lift the line high in the air behind you. This will result in a smoother, straighter presentation. Remember also that the longer the line out behind, the longer the wait at 1:00 before flicking your wrist forward to complete the cast. This timing skill must be practiced to perfect it, but once mastered, it is in my opinion, the key to all fly casting. An easy way to remember where 1:00 is in relation to your body is your right or left ear.

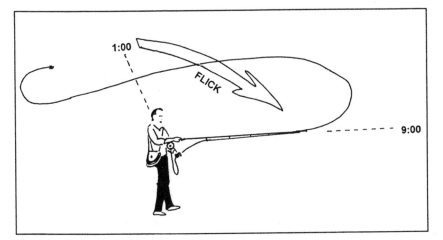

2. Downstroke from 1:00 to 9:00.

The only variation of the forward cast in describing these basic skills is what I term the high arm release. It is used when wishing to present a dry fly, the leader and the line quietly and altogether, thus disturbing skittish trout the least. The clock positions are identical to any standard forward cast, except you finish the cast at 9:00 with your arm raised high and your wrist cocked over in a downward position. Then, with a separate motion, simply drop your arm. You'll be surprised how gently everything reaches the surface of the lake or stream.

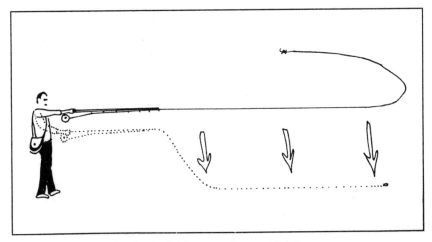

3. Final cast position in the high arm release at 9:00.

EXERCISES

1. Find a place where you have an open field or an open shoreline. Get 15 yards of line out in front of you. The start position will be at 8:30. With a firm upstroke, pick the line up into the air in an upstroke to 1:00 by your ear. Pause momentarily to let the line form its arc and execute the downstroke to 9:00. Practice this straight forward cast, developing a nice fluid motion to the line as it rolls in a large arc behind you and in front. If you hear any snapping you are not pausing enough, and it will usually cost you a fly as it "snaps" off.

2. Practice the high arm release once you have 30-35 yards of line being cast out in a straight line in front. Remember the clock positions are identical to any standard forward cast, except you finish the cast at 9:00 with your arm raised high and your wrist cocked over in a downward position. Then, with a separate motion, simply drop your arm.

Carey Special

Skill 7
The Art of Stripping

The seventh skill to learn is the first of the fishing arts. It is termed stripping. Not to be confused with the age-old art of public disrobing, stripping is simply pulling the cast out fly line toward you in short, erratic and various speed jerks. The objective is to move the fly at the speed common to that of the fish food imitated; be it insect, insect larva or pupa, small fish, leech, shrimp, chironomid or what have you. We now move from basic casting to the skills and arts of basic fly fishing. I have used two key sayings for years to describe both the position of the rod when fishing and the speed of the retrieve. These maxims are "fish in the water" and "speed of a bug."

By fish in the water, I mean that your rod tip should be positioned no higher than 4 inches and preferably 2 inches from the water surface, so it appears as if you are actually fishing in the water.

By speed of a bug I refer to the retrieve speed. It can vary with the fish food imitated, but generally speaking, a slow, erratic retrieve will achieve the best results. In any case, the retrieve speed must imitate whatever food you are offering.

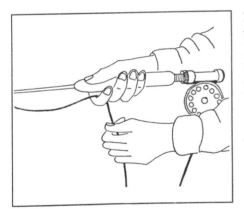

Stripping over the index finger.

Mastering stripping is easy. After the line has been cast out, take the line just ahead of the reel in your free hand and place it over the extended index finger of the hand holding your rod. Next, touch the finger including the line to the forward part of the cork handle. Now open your finger away from the cork slightly to form a "hook."

Now, as you hold the line between the thumb and forefinger of the free hand, pull an inch or two of line from below your finger and release it.

Do not reach ahead of your strip finger or hand to strip in line. Repeat this process until you have a pile of line at your feet and you are ready to cast again or, if you are lucky, a fish takes your offering.

EXERCISES

1. Execute a roll cast to get 20 yards of line out in front. Pick it up into a false cast to get 30-35 yards of line out and to execute the final cast. With the fish in the water and speed of a bug routine, strip the line back over the index finger, simulating a bug movement on or in the water. Remember the rod tip is near the water. Bring in 10 yards of line then execute the false cast to get the line back out and do it again. When you have about 5 feet of line, or more as you improve, left below you try a final shoot at 8:30 to let all of the line "shoot" through the guides.

Elk Hair Caddis

Skill 8
Making and Mending Line

Mastering the eighth skill takes slightly more concentration than stripping. This skill is known by two terms. They are "making line" and "mending line." This tactic is employed whenever stripped-in line must be kept out of the water, particularly when you are standing waist deep in a stream. If the line is allowed to reach the river, the current will carry it downstream, making it impossible to cast. Therefore a method of containing all of the fished-in line in your free hand must be used.

Half way between the reel and the first rod guide grasp the line between your thumb and index finger. Next, rotate your wrist and hand over the line and grip it with the remaining three fingers. At the same time pull two to three inches of line toward you and release your grip with your thumb and index finger, rotating your hand back to its original position, thereby forming a loop in your hand.

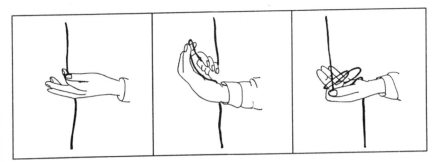

1. Grasp the line between the thumb and forefinger of the free hand, extending the remaining three fingers.

2. Rotate the wrist and hand over the line to push down on 3 inches of line with the three extended fingers and bring the loop into the palm.

3. Release grip with thumb and forefinger rotating your hand back to original position, forming line loops in the palm.

Keep repeating this procedure until the desired amount of retrieved line is achieved. When teaching my students I have shortened making or mending line down to another key phrase, "front two then back three," referring to your fingers and thumb of your rotating free hand. To finish the process, execute a regular forward cast and simply open your hand, palm up, as the rod comes down to 9:00. The result will be that the now freed loops will shoot through the level guides like a rifle barrel, thereby completing the cast.

Skill 9
Fishing the Most Logical Fly for the Occasion

Once you have practiced and, by now, hopefully mastered the previous eight casting and fishing techniques, you are now ready to consider the ninth skill, which I call "fish the most logical fly for the occasion." As previously stated, the artificial flies in your box represent a multitude of fish foods, as well as attractor patterns, which emulate absolutely nothing. This fact affords you an almost unlimited choice of offerings you may present to the trout, salmon or steelhead. Keep in mind that there is no substitute for the knowledge concerning the organisms that fish eat in certain waters at various times of the year. This knowledge will come from four sources: personal experience, reading, watching videos and discussing choices with your fellow fly fisher friends. When fishing a lake or stream for the first time, try your various attractor patterns to catch your first fish. I have found, over many years, that the Royal Coachman tied with polar bear hair or dyed, white deer hair is a sure fire winner in these circumstances. Then, if you intend to keep the fish, examine its stomach contents or, if the fish is to be released, quickly insert a miniature pump available at most fishing and fly shops, down the fish's throat to achieve the same results.

One of the most common questions I get asked in my classes is what fly do I use. This is not surprising, considering the array of flies available. It can be quite overwhelming. I tell people that they really do not need more than ten flies in their fly box. This book would not be complete if I did not suggest a starting kit of flies. The best bet is to experiment with the following table. It is readily acknowledged that the most productive and popular imitations are in this table. I have also indicated the eleven best, in bold.

This table will serve as a guide to help get you started. The patterns will cover a vast majority of insects and other fish foods. As you gain experience, you will try other patterns and methods, but the real skill is in selecting the right time and place...and simulating the bug, or whatever, in the water.

Insect	Stage	Best Time to Imitate	Fly Imitations
Chironomid	Larva	April to May Sept. to Oct.	**Red Bloodworm**
	Pupa	March to July Sept. to Nov.	Chan's Chironomid
	Adult	March to July Sept. to Nov.	Elk Hair Caddis
Mayfly	Nymph	April to July	March Brown **Royal Coachman** Halfback
	Adult	May to July	Adams Royal Wulff **Tom Thumb**
Damselfly	Nymph	May to June	**Doc Sprately** 52 Buick
	Adult	June to July	Marabou Damsel
Dragonfly	Nymph	March to July	**Deer Hair Gomphus**
Caddis Fly	Larva	March to April	Woolly Worm
	Pupa	June to July	Halfback **Carey Special**
	Adult	June to July	Tom Thumb Mitch's Sedge
Water Boatman		March to May Sept. to Oct.	**Water Boatman**
Scuds (fresh water shrimp)		March to April Sept. to Oct.	**Anderson's Shrimp** Werner Shrimp
Leeches		March to April Aug. to Oct.	Marabou Leech **Woolly Bugger**
Minnows		March to April	**Stickleback Minnow**
Eggs		Sept. to Nov.	**Egg & I**

The following table gives you a better idea of what the more popular flies look like.

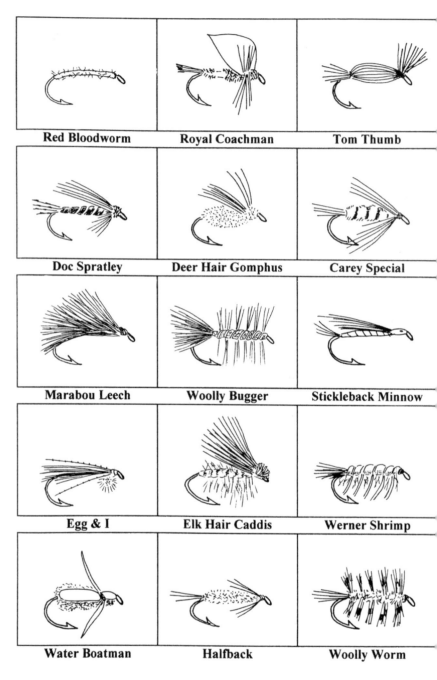

Red Bloodworm	Royal Coachman	Tom Thumb
Doc Spratley	Deer Hair Gomphus	Carey Special
Marabou Leech	Woolly Bugger	Stickleback Minnow
Egg & I	Elk Hair Caddis	Werner Shrimp
Water Boatman	Halfback	Woolly Worm

Skill 10
Major and Minor Fish Feeding Patterns

Skill number ten is a comparatively easy one to learn and is really nothing more than an extension of the one described in Skill 9. I term it "major and minor fish feeding patterns." A classic example of a major would be as follows; coastal sea-run migrating cutthroat trout are 60-70 percent dependent on the movements of Pacific salmon.

Specifically, these trout gorge on roe and single eggs during the fall spawning migration. Conversely as spring approaches and the eggs hatch, these fish scour all coastal streams and sloughs for salmon alevins and fry. (Alevins are a tadpole-looking phase of the fish growth just after the egg hatches.) The second example of a major would be that in the interior of our province, the Kamloops rainbow trout are 60-70 percent dependent on seven forms of adult and immature forms of insect life plus freshwater shrimp, leeches and bloodworms. These insects are damsel and dragonflies, stonefly, mayfly, sedges, chironomids and water boatmen. A minor feeding pattern could be exemplified by both the cutthroat and rainbow trout resident in Buntzen Lake, a BC Hydro managed urban lake near where I live. I have checked the stomachs of dozens of these trout and have found, a 30-40 percent preference for sticklebacks, a small fish with prickly fins seldom exceeding two inches in length.

The following table can be used as a guide to help determine when fish are active and where to go. Use this table with the previous table on suggested flies.

MONTH	ACTIVE FISH	ACTIVE WATERS
JANUARY	Steelhead	Rivers
FEBRUARY	Cutthroat, Steelhead	Spawning in streams
MARCH	Cutthroat, Steelhead	Sloughs and creek mouths
APRIL	Cutthroat	Coastal lakes
MAY	Chinook	Fraser River
	Rainbow	Coastal, interior low-altitude lakes
JUNE	Kamloops Trout	Interior lakes at their best
JULY	Rainbow, Dollys	Lakes and rivers
AUGUST	Chinook	Upper Fraser River bars
SEPTEMBER	Rainbow	Lakes
OCTOBER	Coho, Cutthroat	Rivers and creeks
NOVEMBER	Coho, Cutthroat	Rivers and creeks
DECEMBER	Steelhead	Rivers

Skill 11
Playing and Releasing the Fish

Skill eleven, the playing and releasing of any fish, particularly a small one, is a fairly straight forward procedure. Having hooked the fish, immediately raise the rod to the 12:00 position and begin stripping the fish toward you until your leader appears above the water. Now simply bring the rod past 12:00, over your shoulder, so as to lever the fish to your feet, boat, canoe or float tube. Keeping the fish in the water, reach down and grip the fly, not the fish. With a firm grasp on the hook, tip your wrist, knuckles down and snap in a sharp downward thrust to free the fish. *Using barbless hooks, releasing fish is accomplished with half the effort employed when using barbed ones. The catch and release practice is important to conservation of stock and saving fish for the future.*

Skill 12
Playing and Landing the Fish

The final basic skill is the playing and subsequent landing, boating and netting of larger fish such as river salmon, steelhead and interior Kamloops trout.

Once you have hooked the fish, raise the rod to 12:00 and feed the fish all the stripped-in or mended line in your free hand so as to allow the fish to pull line directly from the reel and through the rod guides. When a large game fish is first hooked it will peel many yards of fly line, even some of your backing, from the reel. Let the fish take all the line it wants, all the while keeping the rod at a high angle and your eyes constantly on the rod tip. If the tip goes down, take your hand off the reel handle and let the fish run. When the tip straightens, it signals that the fish is swimming toward you and could easily jump off because of the slack line. To compensate for a slack line, especially if you are a right-handed caster, switch the rod to your left hand and reel fast with your right. Keep the rod high throughout the fight until the fish is obviously tired. The final step is simply to place your landing net in the water and lead the fish into it head first.

Stickleback Minnow

Final Comments

If you have followed these 12 simple, straightforward procedures with a reasonable amount of repetition you should now be roll casting 35-45 feet. You will also be false casting and forward casting up to 60 feet. Finally you should be fishing by both the stripping and making line methods with modest success. The last two skills, concerning the playing, releasing and landing of fish, particularly large ones, will require considerably more practice. You have to lose a few before you perfect the technique. May you proceed from this point to catch many fishes and release most of them! Fly fishing will take you to some of the most unique and beautiful places on earth.

Oh, and remember one more most important point. Just because you are now a fly fisher do not develop the notion or idea, as some do, that somehow you are a little better or superior in some way to your fellow fishers with whom you share the same waters.

Tight Lines,
Ted Peck

(PS Ted sadly passed away in 2003)

Tom Thumb

Equipment Check List

TACKLE	DESCRIPTION	☑
ROD	8.5-9.5 foot graphite, cork handle, AFTMA 6	
REEL	Single action with interchangeable spools	
BACKING	50 yards, 20# test, braided nylon or dacron	
FLY LINE	WF-6-F floating fly line, weight is 6 or 7	
LEADER	9 foot tapered, size 3X	
	5-7 pound test at the tip	
OTHER	Snap hooks, Tie-Fast, nail clippers	
FLIES	Red Bloodworm	
sizes 6-12	Royal Coachman, both wings and hair	
	Tom Thumb	
	Doc Spratley, green, red or black	
	Deer Hair Gomphus	
	Carey Special, green, red or black	
	Water Boatman	
	Werner Shrimp	
	Stickleback Minnow	
	Egg & I	
	Woolly Bugger	

36

Notes

Egg & I

Notes

Halfback

More HANCOCK HOUSE *fishing titles*

Steelhead
Barry M. Thornton
ISBN 0-88839-370-9
5½ x 8½, 192 pages

Saltwater Flyfishing for Pacific Salmon
Barry M. Thornton
ISBN 0-88839-268-0
5½ x 8½, 168 pages

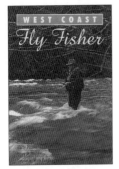

West Coast Fly Fisher
compiled by Mark Pendlington
ISBN 0-88839-440-3
5½ x 8½, 152 pages

West Coast Steelheader
compiled by Mark Pendlington
ISBN 0-88839-459-4
5½ x 8½, 96 pages

Trout Fishing
Ed Rychkun
ISBN 0-88839-338-5
5½ x 8½, 120 pages

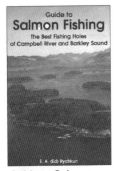

Guide to Salmon Fishing
Ed Rychkun
ISBN 0-88839-305-9
5½ x 8½, 96 pages

Mooching: The Salmon Fisherman's Bible
David Nuttall
ISBN 0-88839-097-1
5½ x 8½, 184 pages

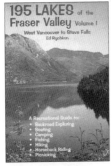

195 Lakes of the Fraser Valley Vol. I
Ed Rychkun
ISBN 0-88839-339-3
5½ x 8½, 238 pages

195 Lakes of the Fraser Valley Vol. II
Ed Rychkun
ISBN 0-88839-377-6
5½ x 8½, 272 pages

HANCOCK HOUSE *natural history titles*

Coastal Wildflowers
ISBN 0-88839-518-3
5½ x 8½, sc, 96 pages

Mountain Wildflowers
ISBN 0-88839-516-7
5½ x 8½, sc, 96 pages

Dryland Wildflowers
ISBN 0-88839-517-5
5½ x 8½, sc, 96 pages

The Bald Eagle
David Hancock
ISBN 0-88839-536-1
5½ x 8½, sc, 96 pages

**Butterflies and Butterfly
Gardening of the
Pacific Northwest**
Mary Kate Woodward
ISBN 0-88839-502-7
5½ x 8½, sc, 96 pages

View all titles at www.hancockhouse.com